M

The Art of Growing Up

By Véronique Vienne with photographs by Jeanne Lipsey

The Art of Growing Up

SIMPLE WAYS TO BE YOURSELF AT LAST

Clarkson Potter/Publishers
New York

Published by Clarkson Potter/Publishers, New York, New York.
Member of the Crown Publishing Group.

Random House, Inc. New York, Toronto, London, Sydney, Auckland
www.randomhouse.com

Printed in Japan

Library of Congress Cataloging-in-Publication Data

Vienne, Véronique.
The art of growing up : simple ways to be yourself at last / by Véronique Vienne ; with photographs by Jeanne Lipsey.—1st ed.
Includes bibliographical references.
1. Adulthood—Psychological aspects. 2. Aging—Psychological aspects. I. Title.
BF724.5 V54 2000
158.1—dc21 00-035975

ISBN 0-609-60739-1

10 9 8 7 6 5 4 3 2 1

First Edition

DEDICATION

To Lilly

ACKNOWLEDGMENTS

In the process of growing up, we become more and more conscious of the talent and generosity of others. First, we would like to thank our editor, Annetta Hanna, whose vision guided the project; our agent, Helen Forson Pratt, who shared our enthusiasm every step of the way; and creative director Marysarah Quinn, for her impeccable taste. Special credits also go to Chelsea Black & White, Margot Schupf, Seamus Mullarkey, Caitlin Daniels, and Sharona Jones for her help in research. We are particularly indebted to the people photographed in these pages, for they were our true inspiration: Bill Young; Marc Pignero; Colette Leconte; Judith Lipsey; Victoria Allen; Kirsten, Michael, and Desmond Turner; Lilly Kilvert; Madeleine Streit; Nelly Della Torre; Raymonde Lanoy; Hélène Mervant; Shelley and Madison Young; Florence Haut; Karen Diefenbach; Peggy Northrop; Carl Lehmann-Haupt; Michael and Sarah Hoffman; Louise, Peter, John and Lexa Harpel; Cheryl Swanson; Kyla Lang; Dodonna Bicknell; Philippe Lechien; Sara Lubtchansky; Edith de Montebello; Cynthia Ryan; Perrine and Léopold Gilles; Emeric, Isabelle, Hugo, and Gaëtan Pinon; Christine and Jean-Jacques de Saint Andrieu; Olivier and Sacha. And hats off to fabulous grown-ups out there, including Phyllis Richmond Cox, Bernie Strassberg, Catherine Ettlinger, Bride Whelan, and Peggy Roalf.

CONTENTS

introduction 9

1 The art of beginning 10
PERSONAL RITES OF PASSAGE 14
Birthday Wishes 19

2 The art of changing 20
DON'T DRAMATIZE 24
Reinventing Adulthood 27

3 The art of cheating 28
THE EASY WAY 33
The Best Age-Defying Beauty Tip Ever 35

4 The art of knowing 36
HOW TO KEEP YOUR MIND ALERT 40
In Defense of Poetry 43

5 The art of shining 44
CREATING A NEW DISCOURSE 48
Never Apologize for Your Age 51

6 The art of inspiring 52
LEAVE IT TO THE IMAGINATION 56
From This Day Forward 59

7 The art of choosing 60
BEYOND THE DUALISTIC APPROACH 63
One Way to Save the World 67

8 The art of succeeding 68
THE MAGIC BULLET 72
The New Rules of Glamour 75

9 The art of laughing 76
THE PURSUIT OF HAPPINESS 81
The Best of Mae West 83

10 The art of becoming 84
THE MYTH 88
The Story of Your Life 91

conclusion 93
a selected bibliography 94
photo credits 96

How old would you be if you didn't know your age?

Life is full of surprises. As we advance in years, we all come to realize that getting older is not synonymous with "not getting younger anymore." In fact, it's exactly the opposite. With each birthday, we experience a delicious increase in vitality, aplomb, and poise.

You certainly look better now than you did twenty years ago.

You definitely wouldn't want to be young again—been there, done that.

And you've finally figured out who you want to be when you grow up. Could it be that each new stage and each new situation in life is an opportunity to shed youthful insecurities, reevaluate old habits, and get rid of obsolete constraints? If that's so, then growing up is, at any age, an amazing process of self-renewal—the legendary fountain of youth we all have been looking for.

This book describes becoming an adult as growing wiser one small realization at a time, from understanding our cells' ability to rebound to appreciating the importance of teaching a child to say good-bye.

Nature, you will learn, is benevolent. Don't try to hold sway over aging with anti-wrinkle creams and pep pills. The second part of your life is not a battleground. Growing up has a lot to do with making things easier on yourself. Like not dramatizing. Being thirty-seven forever. Throwing away musty cookbooks. Choosing your battles. Apologizing rather than making excuses. And figuring out what you do best—then doing it.

1

the art of beginning

Begin anew by throwing away old things. Old shoes, old maps, old cook-books. Outgrowing is part of growing up.

Leave nostalgia to the young. They look best in vintage clothes. Your white leather skirt? Your crepe jumpsuit? Your kimono dress? Pass them on to the next person; let someone else rediscover them. You say you love your old plaid riding jacket? Prove it by

Jacobean & Restoration

Life goes on, but strong
impressions never fade away.

giving it to your favorite nephew.

There is no need to hold on to what's obsolete: One never loses what one tosses away deliberately. Sure, you will probably develop a strong urge to prepare stuffed kohlrabies within a week of getting rid of your copy of *Classic Hungarian Cooking.* But that's to be expected. As soon as you recklessly discard its recipe, that unusual dish you first tasted in Budapest fifteen years ago will seem quite memorable. Absence makes the proverbial heart grow fonder, giving you a chance to savor again a taste you thought was long forgotten.

For every object we cast away, for every friend we lose sight of, for every moment in time we can't recoup, and for every place that's no longer what it used to be, we receive in exchange a wealth of keepsake impressions. How strange—no one can ever take away what is no longer ours.

The richness of your life will depend on how much you've left behind. Apparently out of mind, every precious impression is in fact stored away in the deep recesses of your brain, kept in much better condition than anything stored in your closets, even in mothballs.

Sometimes, strong emotions are preserved in sounds. The mere mention of the name of a distant childhood friend will suddenly summon up his presence in the room. Smells are also wardens of our memories. The scent of baby powder will conjure up the vivid image of your mother as a young woman—looking a lot more vivacious than she ever did in those staid family pictures.

We come of age not by accumulating experiences—"Experience is what you get when you didn't get what you wanted," says the proverb—but by trading impermanent objects for permanent recollections. It's a paradox. In order to keep everything, we have to be willing to let go of it all.

PERSONAL RITES OF PASSAGE

In most aboriginal cultures, rites of passage were first and foremost rites of separation. As cruel as some of these ancient ceremonies seem to us now, their intent was to help people disentangle themselves from the things of the past in order to move into the next phase of their adult life.

Though it could be argued that twenty-year high-school reunions rate up there with some of the most intimidating hazing ceremonies of the Kurnai—a native tribe of southeast Australia known for their long and arcane initiation rituals into adulthood—today traditional rites of passage are no longer deemed necessary. From military service to childbirth, they have become optional. Even the ordeal of waiting in line to renew one's driver's license has been eliminated in most states. Birthdays notwithstanding, we seem to slide from adolescence into maturity without ever being tested.

Too good to be true? You bet. Rites of separation are not extinct, far from it. They have been replaced in our culture by something called "planned obsolescence." In our day and age, we practice detachment constantly as we are forced to discard personal belongings that have been made redundant by our progress-oriented culture.

Our primitive ancestors had to confront their irrational fears of separation when shut up for days in a hut, their faces painted white with clay and their chests tattooed with the blood of a sacred goat. We confront our fears not once during puberty, but all our life, on a daily basis, when trying to decide whether or not to throw away our suddenly outdated laptop computer, our now-unfashionable breadmaking machine, or our formerly hip set of metal chairs.

Parting is still one of the most wrenching of human emotions.

A century ago, many European immigrants had never left their village before going off to America. Unprepared for the experience of parting, they had no farewell rituals, no last-minute bear hugs, no waving of handkerchiefs. Horse-drawn wagons took them away to the train station while the wives and children who stayed behind just stood by, at a loss, a blank expression on their faces.

In contrast, today we learn to handle leave-taking at an early age. Even before we can walk, we are shown how to "say bye-bye." As childish as this waving gesture may seem, it is a critical developmental tool. Though infants are able to grab on to things from birth, not before they are nine or ten months old can they be expected to intentionally release their grip. Showing them how to open their hand to acknowledge someone's departure not only gives them a sense of control of their motor skills, it also eases their separation anxiety.

All through life, the same learning process must be repeated. Over and over, adults must be reminded to open their hands and let go.

In our culture, we confuse rites of separation with disappointments. Growing up is a series of small letdowns. It starts with finding out that there is no Santa Claus, no tooth fairy, no Superman. With each passing year, children come across more occasions for tears—from the family dog's running away to the girl next door's getting the latest pair of sneakers before they do. By the time they reach adolescence, they are likely to have said "That's not fair!" a thousand times.

In reality, this progressive loss of innocence is a blessing, not a curse. Each time a small illusion is taken away, your chances of finding true happiness increase proportionally.

You discover that you are not Daddy's precious little girl after all? Have no regrets. In the next few months, trying to please everyone will become less important to you. As you grow more confident, fortune will smile on you.

Or it soon becomes evident that you are not the femme fatale or the Casanova you thought you were? Cheer up. Swaggering lovers are a bore. You are about to discover the true meaning of romance.

Or, at last, you come to terms with the fact that you are not God's gift to the universe? Bless your heart. Your friends would stop returning your calls if you were.

You begin to grow up when it dawns on you that all your alleged setbacks are in fact opportunities. But don't say "live and learn." Instead, deal with your problems with a healthy dose of "live and *unlearn*" attitude. Curiosity is the best cure for disappointments.

First practice on small annoyances: interruptions, delays, cancellations. Take advantage of these sudden changes of program to take a deep breath and catch up with some of your own sweet thoughts.

Then practice on minor ordeals: clearing up the table, folding the laundry, walking the dog. Turn these mindless tasks into occasions for quiet introspection.

Last but not least, savor apparently insignificant moments when nature itself seems to encourage us to release our grip: when a leaf falls from a tree, when the sun suddenly disappears behind a hill, or when a soft autumn drizzle blurs the landscape.

Make room for the new by letting go gently, one modest realization at a time.

Every beginning is a merging of
holding on and letting go.

Birthday Wishes

We all want love, fame, and fortune. Get specific, though. Next time you blow out your birthday candles, imagine what you would wish for, if you could have it all.

- Lifetime season tickets to the symphony
- Clean windows every day
- More personal discipline
- An eye for collecting rare African art
- A golden Labrador
- A social secretary, a housekeeper, and a cook
- Spiritual understanding
- The time and the money to start an art school
- A good relationship with your children
- Access to smart people
- A pain-free body
- The courage to give up the past
- A private audience with the Dalai Lama
- Argentine tango lessons
- Unexpected joy

The things one wants the most are not things after all.

2

the art of changing

Chances are you were smiling, not frowning, when you noticed your first wrinkle. That silly grin of yours, the one that used to conjure up dimples, is responsible for a new network of fine lines around your eyes. It took 200,000 smiles for you to get crow's-feet, but here you are: a grown-up, albeit a little peeved. Cheer up. These minute changes on your face are evidence that

you have negotiated the first part of your life without major mishap.

- You have outgrown the perils of youth.
- You no longer relish horror movies.
- You know which fork to use.
- You apologize rather than make up excuses.
- You find disappointments a little less disappointing.

Statistically, the most dangerous time to be alive is when you are young. The worst years, particularly for men, are between the ages of eleven and twenty-three. While a woman in her seventies can reasonably expect to live to be ninety, the life expectancy of her newborn grandson is shorter by two decades.

Yet, in our popular culture, we reach the safety of adulthood reluctantly because we assume that each passing year diminishes our physical appeal, reduces our resistance to diseases, and threatens our well-being.

You will be thrilled to hear that this pessimistic view of maturity is not only inaccurate, it has no scientific basis whatsoever. Aging is not an irreversible downward spiral into decrepitude but an affirmation of the principle of self-renewal.

The most fundamental characteristic of living creatures of all sizes—from the smallest mycoplasma to the tallest sequoia—is a mysterious ability to keep rebounding. We and the rest of the vertebrates and invertebrates on this planet are endowed with a lifelong recovery system. Inanimate objects, in contrast, must endure wear and tear without biological recourse.

Now, with genetic engineering the next frontier, the day may come when scientists figure out a way to insert DNA into

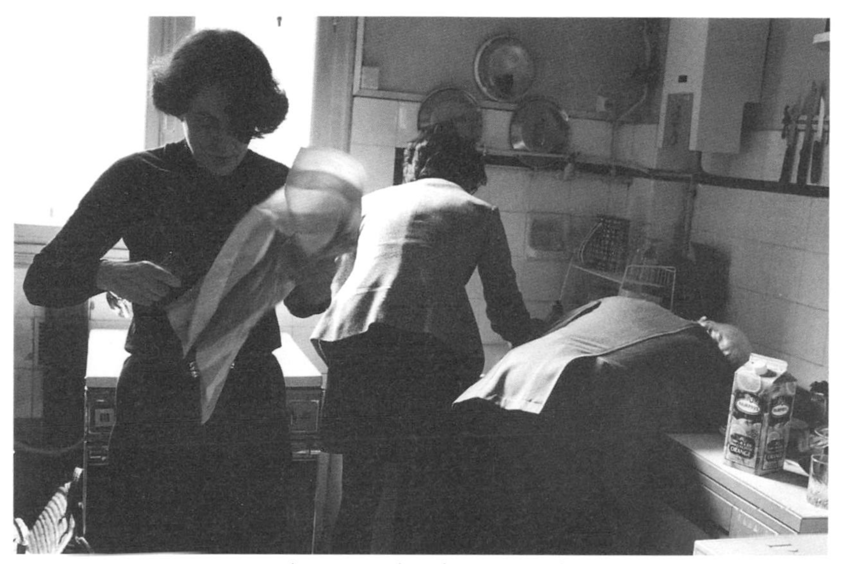

Fixing things and tidying up the mess
is our biological destiny.

lumps of matter. That day, cracked mirrors will mend themselves and faucets will fix their own leaks. While you sleep—and while your own body repairs itself—things around your house will undo whatever damage they have sustained during the day. Even your favorite mug—the one that got badly chipped in the dishwasher the night before—will look practically brand-new by the time you reach for it to hold your morning coffee.

In the meantime, don't fire the repairman: The gift of self-healing is still the unique trademark of living organisms—the one real advantage beings have over inert matter.

Unlike Buddhists who believe that reality is in constant flux, we in the West are still operating under the Platonic assumption that, in the best of all worlds, there is an ideal perfection out there—one free from flaws, errors, or natural cataclysms. If something needs to be fixed, we suspect that the system failed or that someone made a mistake. To emphasize the fact that recovery is necessary only occasionally—after a long illness, a dangerous operation, or an unexpected accident—we celebrate convalescence with get-well cards, flowers, and balloons.

Little do we understand that, at the molecular level, bouncing back is a way of life. Ten thousand times a day, the hundred trillion cells in our body sustain damage from dangerous radicals that rip electrons and atoms from other molecules—and ten thousand times a day, that damage is promptly repaired.

We would simply rust from the inside out like old cars left in the yard if our cells didn't have this uncanny ability to instantly neutralize the powerful oxidants released as a result of respiration. We owe our good health, resilience, and longevity to this constant renewal.

So next time you are running ragged—your knees kill you, your lower back aches, and your waist is thickening—don't gripe against your fate. Roll up your sleeves instead. Rub your hands. Pitch in. To learn to fix things up is your biological destiny.

DON'T DRAMATIZE

Paradoxically, the older you get, the less likely you are to die. Some scientists believe that the aging process occurs later in life to protect us from a premature demise. As we become more careful with age, we are less likely to hurt ourselves, and as our cell growth slows down, diseases develop at a less rapid rate.

Forget coming to terms with your mortality. Life becomes truly precious when you come to terms with your amazing will to live. As far as your body is concerned, quitting is not an option. Only when you gain a healthy respect for the biological determinism of your cells and when you begin to understand the ultimate benevolence of the aging process are you on your way to becoming a compassionate human being.

Mend your broken heart. Only heroes die of love. We survive.
Define progress as taking two small steps forward for each step back.
Don't exaggerate your weaknesses.
Stick to the schedule.
Remember that late is in fact never too late.
Continue what you have begun.
Don't seek closure.

To all of you out there dallying with the mirror, here is the good news: Now that you have made it so far, the best is yet to be. Julia Child wrote her first best-seller at forty-nine; Harry Truman was first elected to the Senate at fifty; Paul Cézanne didn't have a major exhibition until he was sixty-five; and Nelson Mandela became president of South Africa at seventy-five.

As soon as you notice your first wrinkle and your first white hair, sigh with ease. You are well on your way to becoming who you always wanted to be.

This should be fun.

Reinventing Adulthood

Become the kind of grown-up who makes young people wish they were pushing forty, fifty, or even sixty. Let the next generation know that terrestrial tenure improves with age and that getting older gives you permission to be at once funny, stylish, and sincere.

- Dress with flair. Be dapper. Show some style.
- Cook gourmet food for anyone under twenty-one. Give untrained palates something to remember.
- Own beautiful things. A pair of fine handmade leather gloves will bestow a sense of attainment and tranquility no plastic surgery can ever grant you.
- Take piano lessons.
- Have secrets. Keep to yourself the name of your perfume, the cost of your new car, the location of your beach house, the identity of your last lover, and your views on global warming.
- Serve excellent wine, but don't talk about it.
- Build permanent bookcases.
- Use long words around short people. Teach a five-year-old to say "facetious."
- Take a week, a month, or a year, but in the end always patch things up with friends who have angered you.

Think of being up in years as a novelty.

3

The art of cheating

Fools that we are, we pray for a long life but fear old age, says the Chinese proverb. We can't accept that aging is in fact one of nature's kindest trade-offs, and that a touch of dotage is a small price to pay for a long stay on this enchanted planet.

But could it be that we are indeed showing early signs of mental decline when, instead of enjoying

this biological reprieve, we pine for the slim silhouette, the full lips, and the bony knees of folks half our age?

Rather than becoming increasingly disgruntled with our appearance as we go, shouldn't we try to embrace the concept that looking a little older is actually more attractive than looking immature?

First, let's learn to appreciate the beauty of ageful eyes—how much more luminous they are against the soft organza of tiny expression lines.

Then, let's notice the high cheekbones of worldly adults and envy their handsome features no longer buried under baby fat.

Let's not forget to admire the curve of wise lips, held in mysterious suspension—and unlikely to part into some insipid smile.

Last but not least, let's marvel at these finely chiseled furrows that dramatically enhance the character and intelligence of an older face.

Nice try, but no-go. We can't get rid of our ageist notions and convince ourselves that wrinkles and sags are glamorous assets that give us an air of sophistication. Instead, we approach our mirrors, calculator in hand, ready to crunch numbers. We analyze the visual data with the mind of an accountant. Do I still look five years younger? Can I pass for thirty? Would losing four pounds take six years off my face? This is no simple arithmetic, mind you. We must factor in the vanity index and make complex adjustments to account for body type, income bracket, zip code, and hair texture.

We monitor our reflection in the mirror not so much to keep track of inevitable physical changes, but rather to affirm our own sense of timing. Chronological age doesn't reflect the internal reality. Usually a girl is seventeen in her head before she celebrates her thirteenth birthday. When

At long last, you can flaunt
the intelligence of your face.

she turns eighteen, she is insulted when the bartender asks for her ID because he thinks she is sixteen.

Then, at age twenty-five, she changes her mind and stops trying to add years to her appearance. For the next couple of decades, she will look and feel younger than her age. On her thirty-first birthday, she doesn't appear to be a day older than twenty-four. At forty-five, she feels thirty-seven—a figure that will reflect her mindset for many more years to come.

At sixty, she may reluctantly turn fifty. Then, at sixty-five, she will do another about-face and tell her new girlfriends at the club that she is a perky seventy-one. A decade later, pretending to be a dapper ninety-something, she'll wonder how she got to be so old so quickly.

For a man, carbon dating is a lot easier. The minute male friends begin to compliment him on his youthful appearance, he can be sure that his looks are no longer what they used to be. But as long as he feels that old is fifteen years older than he is, he will never be elderly.

We can thank Einstein for this state of affairs. Time, he discovered, is relative to the way we measure it. Your biological clock, the drift of continents, the program of your cells, your watch, and the calendar on the wall measure different times. Furthermore, how we perceive duration is affected by the number of stimuli we receive during a given period. Objectively speaking, time is subjective. So, don't worry: You are the age you say you are—no ifs, ands, or buts about it.

Lady Windermere, one of Oscar Wilde's fictional characters, never admitted that she was more than twenty-nine, or thirty at the most. "Twenty-nine when there are pink shades, thirty when there are not," she explained.

Fifty is the age of elegance.

So pick an age you feel comfortable with and stop fretting. You can be thirty-seven forever if you choose. Forty-two has its advantage too: It's mature yet alluring. Recently, fifty-one has been gaining popularity with the smart set.

Once you've figured out how old you are, stay with it. Make that number the basis of your style. Explore all its possibilities. Reinvent the category if you must, to keep up with changing trends and lifestyles. Cheat even, if it comes to that. Just don't combine pantsuits with bleached-blond highlights, and you'll be fine.

THE EASY WAY

Get used to the idea that you will never be old, no matter what your passport says. You will always feel younger (and less experienced) than most of your contemporaries. Younger (and less serious) than the people who were in kindergarten when you were in high school. Younger (and more optimistic) than your friends' children, even though some of them now have jobs on Wall Street.

Don't worry, though: Feeling younger doesn't exclude being a grown-up. You can be a kid at heart and still be a complete adult, fully functional, possessing all the moral, spiritual, and ethical niceties such as patience, dependability, and compassion.

Growing up has very little to do with age. The fact that we think it does is what makes the process so unattractive to young adults. As a result of this misconception, they wait and procrastinate, as if acting juvenile as long as possible could delay the eventual onset of senility.

In fact, you become a grown-up when you realize that age brought you no wisdom you couldn't have gotten on your own ten or even twenty years earlier.

You become a grown-up when you realize that you don't have to find the hardest way to get things done. When you wish you had learned to cook by simply watching your mother in the kitchen. When you don't hyperventilate because your haircut is a little too short. When you buy yourself the best handsaw money can buy. When you move your computer out of your bedroom. And when you let the makeup artist at the cosmetics counter show you her beauty tips.

Delay maturity as long as you need to, but remember that whenever you are ready to join the human race, growing up will be a breeze. The ultimate power trip is not to resist adulthood, as some youth culture marketers would have us believe.

The ultimate power trip is to make your life easier.

The Best Age-Defying Beauty Tip Ever

Smile*

* Unfortunately, you can't cheat. Simply lifting the corners of your mouth will not take years off your face. Only sincere smiles, complete with crinkling eyes, trigger waves of activity in the left prefrontal lobe of your brain where happiness resides.

4

the art of knowing

One of the advantages of growing up is that no one tells you anymore that you are too smart for your own good. The days when your intelligence used to get you into trouble are over. You are among your peers at long last, and everyone is at least as clever as you are. In such good company, men can stop acting dense and women don't have to be coy any longer. For that reason

Self-inquiry is a matter of survival.

alone, adulthood is a lot of fun. As John F. Kennedy used to say, "You can't beat brains."

Your brain, on the other hand, will always try to beat you at your own game.

It goes this way: You greet a colleague with the customary "You look great today." As luck would have it, it happens to be a particularly bad hair day for your coworker, and your innocent compliment sounds unexpectedly ironic. In a flash, you consider your options: Add an earnest remark, smile warmly, or simply ignore the slight gaffe and move on.

Uninvited, an inner voice cuts in and notes wryly that *we flatter others in order to be flattered in return.* Before you can delete this unpleasant comment, an internal discussion arises, with your mental circuitry firing suggestions and criticisms right and left. *What's this obsession with looking great, anyway? Quick, make a self-deprecating remark. Suggest lunch. Who ever said "Learn to be sincere even if you have to fake it?"*

Don't take it personally. It's only your mind talking to you.

Day in and day out, a democratic process takes place inside our heads, with every cortical cell voicing its opinion freely. Our ten billion neurons and sixty trillion synapses respond instantly to every electrical impulse coming from every corner of the brain.

Traveling along common nerve pathways—converging, overlapping, interconnecting—our thoughts keep no secrets from one another. As a result, a provocative internal dialogue goes on—and on, and on—whether or not we know it, or choose to listen to it.

"Nothing was ever so unfamiliar and startling to me as my own thoughts," wrote Thoreau.

This constant cerebral badinage is

unnerving, particularly when you are young. The quirkiness of some of these impromptu comments can undermine your self-confidence. With time, though, you learn to appreciate the irreverent tone of these unsolicited and fugitive mental footnotes. Acting as your inner jester—cracking jokes and making faces at you when you least expect it—your mind encourages you to question your most comfortable assumptions.

For our species, repeated self-examination is a matter of survival. We didn't evolve by taking things for granted, by accepting the given. With the same brain that our sapiens ancestors used to hunt mammoths and live through the rigors of the last Ice Age, modern humans have taught themselves to fox-trot, play poker, fold damask napkins in the shape of swans, perform laser surgery to reattach severed fingers, hack into Secret Service computer files, and execute flawless triple-axel jumps.

So don't pretend to be clueless ever again. Like most people, you probably underestimate your mental capacities. From now on, simply assume that you know things you don't even know you know. When you run into a new problem, instead of asking others for recommendations, suggestions, or permission to proceed, trust your wits. First assume that you are the best person for the job. Your brain has been engineered to solve the future riddles of humanity.

HOW TO KEEP YOUR MIND ALERT

You don't have to reinvent the wheel in order to keep your neurological pathways in working order. What you do have to do, though, is invent new ways of thinking about the same old things. In doing so, you create new electrical signals that transit through your central nervous system along synaptic roads less traveled.

Creating new connections between existing neurons is how the brain repairs, maintains, and regenerates itself. There is also new evidence that human beings can grow new cortical cells well into old age. Even our spinal cord is smarter than we think: When accidentally cut off from the brain, it can, in some cases, be taught to initiate voluntary movements on its own.

Increasing our vocabulary is one way we can strengthen our mental circuitry. When we call a dog "man's best friend," for instance, or when we talk about getting married as "taking a trip down the aisle," we unknowingly invigorate our brain. The more complex the imagery of the metaphor, the more active our synapses. So go ahead, curl up between the sheets, shake a leg, bite the bullet, feed the devil with a long-handled spoon, or, as they say in the rural South, grin like a fox eating yellow jackets —it's good for you.

For the same reason, don't snub colloquialisms, jargon, psychobabble, cyber-speech, political euphemisms, street slang, or even annoyingly trendy expressions such as "differently abled," "infoglut," or "attitude-rich." Say it with a chuckle. It's all fuel for your thinking machine.

Stay on the cultural edge by talking about category killers instead of cheap products and by giving people your street coordinates instead of your address. Do it for the fun of it—not to be pompous—and no one will ever think that you are matronly, mature, quaint, stodgy, square, corny, replaceable, rinky-dink, or, God forbid, "distinguished."

In Defense of Poetry

The English language is full of poetic figures of speech that can engage your imagination and boost the activity in your brain. Neither proverbs nor clichés, they are what poets called *tropes*—figurative expressions that deepen the meaning of things by unexpectedly conjuring up visual sensations tucked away in the recesses of your mind.

Attributed to the likes of Shakespeare, Marlowe, and Robert Louis Stevenson, among others, many of the following expressions make allusions to ancient traditions. Use them from time to time, and make poetry part of your life.

- A face that launched a thousand ships (a very beautiful woman)
- An Iliad of woes (all the calamities of the world)
- The last infirmity of a noble mind (the desire for fame)
- In two shakes of a lamb's tail (in hardly any time at all)
- Knee-high to a grasshopper (small)
- Quicker than hell can scorch a feather (fast)
- To fiddle while Rome burns (to ignore a crisis)
- To flutter the dovecote (to cause confusion)
- To walk the chalk (to obey the rules)
- To wear calluses on your elbows (to hang around in bars)
- To know a hawk from a handsaw (to know what's what)
- To syncopate the long hand (to be late)

For each new word we learn, we create a thousand mental connections.

5

the art of shining

Like the planet on which we live, we bask in a shimmer of reflected light: We shine in the eyes of others. But sooner or later, even the most radiant among us will experience a temporary eclipse. As we get older, invisibility becomes more of a problem. With young people genetically programmed to steal the show, eventually all adults will find themselves unexpectedly ban-

ished from the front row of life.

No wishful thinking can make us conspicuous when the world doesn't seem to notice our presence. Women sometimes try eye-catching tricks such as rattling their jewelry or striking a pose. Men prefer sulking to draw people's attention. But such stopgap measures seldom restore our visibility.

With time, though, we eventually learn to come to terms with these existential episodes during which we can see everyone—but no one can see us. A successful reappearing act requires we change not so much the way we look, but the way others look at us.

It is a well-known fact in scientific circles that most of us are likely to see only what we expect to see, regardless of what is actually before us. Our preconceived ideas shape our perceptions. It has to do with the way our optical nerves are connected to our cerebral cortex: Familiar shapes and straightforward colors, which engage fewer cognitive resources, are easily perceived by our brain, whereas freeforms and in-between tints are likely to be dismissed as a blur. We become invisible when the viewer's brain cannot process the visual contradictions that we unwittingly present to him or her.

Take a well-established surgeon wandering into a crowded downtown gallery during an opening. He might as well be a fly on the wall: He has slipped out of other people's field of vision because he is not part of the ultracool art crowd.

How about the dedicated mother of two who is overlooked for a major promotion at work in spite of her stellar performance? Her boss should be declared "partially sighted." He cannot see how someone who is an expert at making peanut-butter sandwiches can also be a good corporate officer.

Become visible by stepping out of other people's blind spot.

When women do not acknowledge their appreciative glances, mature men feel invisible too, as if they were looking at the world through a dark one-way mirror. The female of the species has her blind spots. She is likely to treat older admirers like mere insects rather than consider the possibility that nice gents sporting bow ties can also be potential suitors.

Making matters worse for all of us, invisibility is a private ordeal, one we cannot share with others, alienated as we feel in this predicament. But we have only ourselves to blame for this situation. Consciously or not, we all make one another feel invisible at times. With unseeing glances, we send some of the best among us scurrying into virtual hiding.

Becoming mindful of how we dismiss people who do not fit the familiar visual stereotypes can teach us how not to fall into invisibility ourselves. The first step is to learn to see beyond the usual clichés. But don't kid yourself, this is not an easy undertaking. Your compassion alone cannot do the job. Honoring the uniqueness in all individuals requires tremendous mental focus.

Seeing and being seen takes keen intelligence. You have to be astute enough to debunk the platitudes that mask your individuality—and the individuality of people around you.

CREATING A NEW DISCOURSE

In the past, adults of all ages formed a staid and homogenous group that was easy to identify. They wore darker clothes and behaved with more restraint and dignity than their younger counterparts. In contrast, the latest generation of grown-ups seems to go out of their way to defy the comfortable conventions of adulthood. Some folks in their sixties emulate people twenty years younger, even as others in their fifties act and look as if they were ready to cash in their chips and buy a motor home.

No one can tell how old anyone is anymore, which is a good thing in many ways. But as age becomes less of a defining factor in human relations, we have yet to find other criteria to help us organize our visual perceptions, decode their meaning, and decide how to act accordingly.

We have to replace the old clichés about aging with brand-new concepts that do not relegate any of us to invisibility.

There are very few pointers. Even the Webster's dictionary has trouble defining the word "adult." An adult is described as (1) fully developed and mature, *and* (2) dealing in or with sexually explicit material. Good grief. Better not count on lexicographers for guidance. To be an adult is to be on one's own.

Instead of trying to change our behavior (in other words, instead of trying to act "young"), we only need to develop a new way of recounting our experience as we move into adulthood. For starters, let's not talk about growing old. Let's find a new language to describe adulthood—this postgraduate age of consent, this exciting half century of continual growth wedged between our salad days and our sunset years.

Let it be known that we love our age. We are, after all, a smart, generous, secure, funny, mysterious, grateful, and snazzy group of folks. So stand your ground. Refuse to be labeled. And don't be intimidated by young women who don't make eye contact when they smile at you or by big men who act as if they don't see you. It's their loss, not yours.

Never Apologize for Your Age

Don't worry about appearing stodgy, old-fashioned, or bossy around members of a younger generation. Never project your own ageist insecurities—defensiveness is a sure way to make others feel uneasy.

- Decide once and for all never to apologize for your age.
- Don't pressure anyone to like you by being overly congenial.
- For the first ninety seconds of a conversation, slow down slightly to give others a chance to feel comfortable with you.
- Ask simple questions at first, and listen attentively to the answers.
- Laconic answers mean that younger people are intimidated by you. Adjust your body language to show that you are accessible. Uncross your arms, stretch your legs, and lean back slightly.
- Don't always agree. Your listener will be stimulated by the different perspective life has given you.
- Let younger people know that you enjoyed meeting them, but don't seek closure by making definite plans to meet again. Allow them to get back to you in their own time.

The secret of eternal youth?
Cultivate the art of never complaining.

6

the art of inspiring

To be a muse is to know all there is to know about love. Instead of trying to figure out What Women Want, or Why Men Don't Call, simply learn to inspire your loved one to write a poem, for instance. Bring out his or her creativity, and do away with relationship advice columns.

The artistic predisposition is in all of us, encoded in our DNA, waiting for the right signal to

Reckless love inspires reckless creativity.

manifest itself. That signal is usually delivered by a heady hormonal brew. "At the touch of love, everyone becomes a poet," said Plato. Sudden infatuation activates our ability not only to write poetry, but also to embellish, adorn, paint, dance, sing, and make music. Like Sleeping Beauty, our creative powers lay dormant in our cells, only to be awakened from their slumber by the biochemical kiss of love.

Mature cells are just as likely as young cells to respond to this dopamine-induced high in ways that are both delicious and surprising. The resulting amorous frisson—that strange levity, that sweet bewilderment—can affect anyone, regardless of age. But the older we get, the more satisfying this poetic awakening is.

While younger lovers are likely to fritter away this surge of creativity in ingenious rendezvous schemes, more experienced paramours will turn romantic episodes into opportunities to grow up. Passion will soon wane, they know, unless they can capitalize on these unexpected jolts of chemistry to express their deepest feelings and encourage their mate to do the same.

Inspiring someone can be as simple as listening. Eavesdrop on the great and wise things your lover says unwittingly, and you will not only buoy up his or her creativity, you will also sharpen your own wit. So much brilliance in this world is lost upon those who have no ears.

Crushes make you more perceptive. With the same wild energy that compels you to dance till dawn in the arms of your beloved, sign up for a class on The English Novel, on French Art Deco, or on Japanese Brush Painting. Those higher levels of testosterone and estrogen enhance your capacity for absorbing new information—on probably a lot less sleep.

Love is an incentive for reaching beyond our usual capacities. Even the simplest gesture, such as sending flowers to your Valentine, can be interpreted as a creative act with momentous consequences. Some anthropologists, in fact, argue that the dawn of humanity can be traced back to a bouquet of flowers left in a prehistoric grave site in northern Iraq 100,000 years ago! If indeed the fossilized pollen of hollyhocks, grape hyacinths, bachelor's buttons, and yellow wildflowers found in that cave were gathered intentionally—not blown together accidentally by the wind—evolution theorists infer that our heavy-browed ancestors were part of the human race.

The ability to express love, yearning, or sadness with something as abstract as a bouquet of flowers proves a capacity for symbolic thought. That first-ever Neanderthal flower arrangement suggests that early humanoids already had a sophisticated system of beliefs about individuality, love, family, and the meaning of life.

In the meantime, back in the twenty-first century, the scientific community would have us believe that falling in love is first and foremost a neurochemical event designed to ensure the survival of our species. If it were so, infatuation would be limited to people in their reproductive prime. But the history of the world proves that no one is ever too old to feel the earth move under his or her feet.

Is the object of the mating dance the mate—or is it the dance?

There is no way of knowing for sure. Causes and effects are often impossible to tell apart. Maybe someday we will revise some of our basic assumptions about human existence and realize that we are driven to pursue a mate not so much to pass on our DNA to the next generation but to experience, as Elizabeth Barrett Browning puts it, "the depth and breadth and height/My soul can reach."

LEAVE IT TO THE IMAGINATION

What makes you sexy has very little to do with the way you look—with or without clothes on—but everything to do with the way you look at life.

Sexiness is a combination of two opposite qualities: determination and spontaneity. A love potion is very often a heady mix of efficiency and surprise. Purposefulness alone, though attractive, is not enough to turn someone on. But throw in a dash of ambiguity, an erotic "maybe," or an enticing "why not?" and you are on your way to creating an exquisite and irresistible sense of expectation.

The greatest romantic figures are go-getters who are willing, from time to time, to be sidetracked to satisfy the whims of their loved ones.

As Claudette Colbert once said: "Plans are one thing, life is another." Be as determined as you must in order to reach your goals—take charge with a can-do attitude—but let it be known that there is always room for improvisation.

A woman can drive a man to distraction by hinting that she might change her mind at the last minute.

A man will win a woman's heart by intimating that he could drop everything for her—were she to insist.

Never make it overt, though. The more subtle the innuendo, the more enticing its promise.

Practice being sexy without ever changing your behavior. Change your way of thinking instead.

When entering a room, for instance, don't decide in advance how you are going to handle the situation. Allow your vulnerability to show through. When talking with someone of the opposite sex, don't try to assess whether or not the person is attracted to you. Savor the moment of indecision. Go with the flow. And if the mood turns flirtatious, leave as much as possible to the imagination.

From This Day Forward

- Looking for Cupid is a sure way not to find him.
- Everyone else will know you are in love before you do.
- Don't take rejection personally. It's never about your shortcomings.
- If a man says, "I am not worthy of your love," don't contradict him. He knows what he is talking about.
- Saying "I love you" is not about words, but about timing.
- Getting married is the best preparation for being married.
- The more intimate you are, the more space you give each other.
- Take sincere compliments with as much poise as unfair criticism.
- Remember that love confers you no rights.

7

the art of choosing

Proof of the superiority of man over beast, we have learned to discriminate among a multitude of kindred options without trepidation. In contrast, some say that a donkey confronted with two identical buckets of water is likely to get confused and die of thirst.

The more you learn about choosing, the easier it gets to tell the difference between real desires and

false preferences. We do it all the time in the name of freedom of choice—we routinely sort through dozens of nearly identical products in order to find the one we like. Far from being a mere expression of acquisitiveness, shopping is a ritual in self-government, a brave daily exercise in ballot-casting.

By the time a woman reaches the age of thirty-five, for instance, picking the very best lipstick out of the hundred and fifty brands currently on the market no longer represents a challenge for her. At long last, she's figured out that all lipsticks are pretty much alike—and so she buys them with abandon. In fact, you can almost pinpoint the exact moment you become an adult to the first time you realize there isn't such a thing on this earth as "the very best" of anything.

Bless the day you discover that good is good enough, and excellence too onerous. Why go out of your way to get the best? Why spoil everything? Life is sweet when the best is yet to be.

Instead of pursuing the peerless and the perfect, use your well-honed choosing skills to reinvent yourself and defy the limitations of your heredity. "The first thing to do is to arrange to be born in Paris," once quipped the flamboyant fashion despot Diana Vreeland. With that one remark, she managed to flaunt and mock all at once her not-so-good fortune. Although *she* was born in Paris, and with wealthy aristocratic parents besides, she was rather homely—by her own account "an ugly little monster."

But biology is not destiny. Diana Vreeland became one of the most stylish, witty, and attractive women of her century by choosing to be not French, but American; not awkward, but elegant; not old-world, but stubbornly modern. Like her, we can reinvent ourselves with the knowledge that whatever happens next is our responsibility. We will never be victims of circumstances as long as we choose to own up to our present flaws and future fumbles.

As we get older, we might as well embrace the poor choices we made decades ago. So be it! Our least brilliant decisions have shaped our future. But it's not all bad news. In fact, in hindsight, some of our worst blunders were strokes of genius.

You married the wrong mate, for instance, but you have terrific children from this union. You labored for half a decade on a useless Ph.D. in anthropology, but you are a better lawyer for it.

The cumulative effect of years of good and bad personal decisions affect every aspect of our lives—and the lives of others. We are our brothers' keepers. As the Dalai Lama would say, we are accountable nation to nation, human to human, and people to all sentient beings. Today, even the weather is our universal responsibility. With global warming an issue, when it's too hot, too cold, too dry, or too wet—when the rain in Spain stays mainly in the plain—we can no longer profess unimpeachability.

We can't choose our heredity, but take heart: We can choose our mistakes and in doing so, we can take full credit for the inscrutable prospect of tomorrow.

BEYOND THE DUALISTIC APPROACH

The relentless search for the best is not a pursuit of excellence, but an attempt to create a duality between what's on top and what's on the bottom, who gets the award and who doesn't, what's progress and what's not.

It all begins in childhood. When asked "Do you want to go to the playground?" two-year-olds find out quickly what fun it is to say "No." You can't blame them. First right of refusal buys them time. As long as they can dig in their heels, the little tyrants are in control. "No," they discover, gives them a chance to think things over, review their options, and anticipate unpleasant consequences.

In other cultures, toddlers are never given the option to say "Yes" or "No." Parents spare their babies the agony and the hubris of personal decision. But this is America, where we believe in teaching our offspring the importance of exercising their right to individual choices.

By the time they are four, children are ready for the next step: the right-versus-wrong conundrum. This dualistic concept is the source of great anxiety for both parents and kids. To this day, no one has been able to explain once and for all how to choose between "right" and "wrong," between "right" and "not wrong," or between "wrong" and "not right." One hundred and fifty years ago, Alexis de Tocqueville came close when he remarked that, in this country, what is useful is seldom deemed wrong. In contrast, what is right is seldom described as convenient, advantageous, or good for the bottom line.

After puberty, adolescents are drawn into the innermost circle of dualistic hell when they are expected to choose good over bad in peer-pressured situations. But, reluctant to play eeny, meeny, miny, mo with one more abstract notion, they are likely to take drastic shortcuts. What feels good, they reckon, is illegal, whereas what feels bad isn't.

And so, with moral dichotomy as their guide, we throw our children out of the nest —out of the frying pan and into the fire.

Personal differences can be shared in unison.

It's only later, between the ages of thirty and forty, that young adults come to terms with the fact that one does not shape one's destiny by answering a series of yes-or-no, right-or-wrong, and good-or-bad questions. That's the grand illusion. Life is a multiple-choice test.

With this realization, children turn into grown-ups. They become our peers, and we get to sit down with them to share a chuckle or two as we compare notes on how we all got there. At that moment, in a burst of conviviality, we all join together as one and the same generation.

One Way to Save the World

One way to save the world is to stash it away in your mind.

Be the eyewitness of all you see.

Don't miss a thing.

Be there when nothing can console the crying baby.

Stay put even though a friend has offended you.

Don't look away when someone needs help.

Be the designated observer of both grief and wonder.

Check the view from the top of the Empire State Building.

Go to Rome. Or Jerusalem. Or Mecca.

Sit for hours on the terrace of a Paris café.

Take an imprint of all these moments and hide them
where only you know.

Then take very good care of yourself.

You are the world's pantry; its reading room; its treasure cave.

"Nothing is lost. All that you have ever seen is always with you."
—Henri Cartier Bresson

8

the art of succeeding

ou know that you are on your way up when you get genuine pleasure from your friends' successes. Instead of hiding behind a potted plant when your school chum gets his third award, you press forward to the front row to be the first to shake his hand as he steps down from the podium.

You don't just send flowers when your ex-

Celebrating the successes of friends and peers becomes second nature.

assistant becomes vice president of your division—you tell her in person how proud you are of her promotion.

And you don't try to look priggish the day your bratty baby sister marries a billionaire. You get yourself the best-looking outfit you can find and have a ball.

Don't be a stranger to success by acting estranged around successful people. Be the human face that greets good fortune. Be the winning presence when others make good.

This is not altruism. We learn to become successful by sharing with others their personal triumphs. High achievements are never anyone's private property. We might as well assume that we own a piece of everyone's successes, because we do. The long and tedious litanies of thanks at award ceremonies are proof enough that moments of victory belong to all of us.

As you advance in years, enjoying other people's successes by proxy feels more and more natural. By the time you are forty, cheering friends and peers in their hour of glory has become second nature. In the process, you've turned into a great emcee. You are second to none as maid of honor. You deserve a gold medal as a toastmaster. And you have hosted more birthday parties than you care to remember.

Thus and so we come of age, all along applauding and clinking glasses to celebrate the great deeds of people whose fame and fortune we share vicariously. As the saying goes, it takes twenty years to become an overnight success—twenty years spent attending a multitude of fêtes and functions. When it's our turn to be lionized—it usually happens the day we learn that the dog needs surgery and that the co-op board has rejected our latest bid for the duplex—we would be just as happy skipping our own jubilee. "By the time we've made it, we've had it," said Malcom Forbes.

In wealthier nations, making it means more than financial rewards. Cross-cultural studies that attempt to chart predictors of life satisfaction have shown that the richer you become, the more difficult you are to please. Make a killing on Wall Street, and idiosyncratic values such as self-actualization and self-esteem move to the top of your must-have list—ahead of security and safety. In other words, by the time you have it all, having it all is too little too late.

The true measure of your success is not how much money you have, or even how much satisfaction you get from your work, how helpful you are to people in need, or how respected you will be after you are gone. In fact, the true measure of your success is not about you. But to find out what makes it all worthwhile, you have to attend one of those potentially embarrassing affairs where you are the featured guest of honor.

It could be an intimate dinner between old friends, or it could be a big charity event. You may be ready for a good time or you may dread the occasion. People might simply raise their glass to you or they might be compelled to give you a standing ovation. It makes no difference. At some point it will hit you: *These folks are enjoying themselves because of who they think I am, not because of me*. At that moment, your success will belong to them, not to you.

You've made it when you are humbled by the realization that your friends and acquaintances derive real pleasure from appreciating you.

THE MAGIC BULLET

Becoming successful could be as simple as taking a pill. If the drug companies didn't have to conform to prickly governmental requirements, they could take advantage of the astonishing placebo effect and sell harmless dummy capsules that could boost our performance, help us focus our ambition, and make winners out of you and me.

If you are skeptical, think again. In controlled experiments, 90 percent of the improvements reported by patients taking Prozac were also reported by patients taking placebos. The best results came when neither patients nor doctors were aware that some of the pills were fake (thus the "double-blind" name of this type of testing procedure).

Pulling off such a benevolent scam would therefore require that physicians be fooled as well. They would have to believe that the drug they prescribe, not their wish to heal people, is the active ingredient in their treatments. If that were to happen, snake oil could have what clinical researchers called "a pre-goal attainment positive effect"—it could activate the area in the left prefrontal cortex associated with ambition, curiosity, and the desire for achievements.

For us, this means that success is always within reach. Self-doubt is the only obstacle between us and easy street. We could get what we want if we had the confidence to imagine reaching our goals. As the medical profession has found out in the last few years, high achievers who trust their skills are happier, healthier, and less likely to have a heart attack than people who worry all the time about whether they can deliver the goods.

As we get older, there seems to be more and more work to do. Let this be an incentive to anticipate success. Nurture in yourself what Jane Austen described as "that sanguine expectation of happiness which is happiness itself." Enjoy the endeavor, and good fortune will come as a result.

Glamour means looking glamorous
even though no one is looking at you.

The New Rules of Glamour

"Glamour" is just another word for a little extra discipline.

- It's knowing how to choose a hat, clean paintbrushes, and effortlessly negotiate a grand marble staircase in a tight evening gown.
- It's treating everyone the way you want to be treated.
- It's never holding a meeting that lasts more than thirty minutes.
- It's figuring out what you do best—and doing it.
- It's wearing off-the-rack clothes as if they were made for you.
- It's acquiring a quirky taste for exotic cuisine, good tuxedos, proper wineglasses, foreign languages, hair ornaments, French bulldogs, and watercolor illustrations.
- It's never suspecting that anyone is jealous.
- It's being weary of generalizations.
- It's closing your eyes when you kiss.
- It's replacing youth with mystery.

the art of laughing

While soaking in your bathtub, you discover that who you are is who you always wanted to be—a much nicer person than the big shot you could have become if you had been a little more flashy. As a sense of relief washes over you, you sink below the bubbles to chortle privately.

Live long enough, and laughing at yourself will become an exquisite treat.

Make them laugh by keeping a straight face.

Being the butt of your own private jokes can also be the source of unexpected comfort. Let's say you just gave what is probably the worst presentation of your career at a business seminar. When the lights come up, you realize that most people sneaked out in the dark and the room is practically empty. You briefly consider slashing your wrists, but end up laughing instead, as the good judgment of your audience strikes you as hilarious.

More often than not, disquieting truths about ourselves prod our sense of humor. The sudden deflation of our ego creates an internal vacuum that triggers a moment of sheer levity. We are visited by laughter when our finite view of reality is replaced, for a brief shining moment, by the infinite wonder of our befuddlement.

Zen practitioners, who savor derision as a way of life, believe that laughing out loud is the only way to reconcile our wish to attain enlightenment with our repeated failure to do so. Rather than fall prey to their sense of grandiosity, they prefer to ridicule their own spiritual achievements.

"You grow up the day you can have your first real laugh—at yourself," said silver-screen legend Ethel Barrymore. True, young people are not amused by their own foibles—they don't get the cosmic joke. They think that being serious, miserable even, makes them more attractive. And sure enough, a single guy who sits by himself at the bar looking dejected is more likely to score with lonely hearts than the grinning idiot who buys everyone a drink.

Apparently, glee is an acquired taste. Did you notice that paintings by old masters never featured people laughing or even smiling? Our museums are full of portraits of young adults doing their very best to look dour. Presumably, in the days before sanitation and antibiotics, too few people lived long enough to develop a sense of humor. Joviality was restricted to banquet scenes, when, under the pretext of inebriation, it was acceptable to be in high spirits. But even then, women were never supposed to chuckle. Men assumed—rightly so, perhaps—that a woman who laughs openly is laughing at them.

During the Renaissance in Europe, with Puritanism on the rise, too much happiness was deemed inappropriate. Laughter was treated as a disease. People prone to hilarity were sometimes bled four ounces, morning and evening, for a week or two, or until they were too weak to titter and kid around.

Today, we go to the other extreme. Comedy is touted as the miracle cure. Research shows that having a good laugh releases opiates and boosts our immune system by increasing the amount of infection-fighting proteins in the bloodstream. So much so that doctors are probably tempted to prescribe humor instead of painkillers. Watch two reruns of *I Love Lucy* and call me in the morning.

Mirth is the one contagious disease that's welcomed by the medical profession. When manipulated into a chuckle, people willy-nilly end up feeling better. Sometimes even fake smiles and canned laughter can do the trick. Physicians are now encouraged to buoy up their bedside manner to speed up their patients' recovery. In hospitals and clinics coast to coast, joviality makes the rounds.

Embracing the healing power of laughter—especially at ourselves—is for those among us who can accept the reality of both truth and exaggeration, joy and misery, success and failure. You can't see the humor in your own situation unless you acknowledge your innate contradictions—something our forefathers found apparently difficult to do.

But where there is contradiction, there is debate. Today, no one can agree whether laughing increases longevity or whether it's the other way around. Indeed, could it be that aging is the reason we can laugh away sickness? Since the older we get, the more likely we are to poke fun at ourselves, we can infer that the older we get, the more likely we are to feel better.

THE PURSUIT OF HAPPINESS

Human beings have a monopoly on laughter. Angels do not laugh; neither do beasts. Devils, on the other hand, love to laugh at us—mocking us for trying to claim happiness as a prerogative and a privilege. Snickering demons, they know that the more satisfaction we expect from life, the more likely we are to run into disappointments.

Granted, our dreams and hopes are often ridiculous. But we can have the last laugh if we pursue happiness for the pleasure of the pursuit, not for its fleeting benefits. Ask people who have it all and they'll tell you: They were never as happy as when they were on their way to the top.

Like true happiness, true humor is what happens before the punch line. "The test of a real comedian is whether you laugh at him before he opens his mouth," said drama critic George Jean Nathan.

Have the first laugh and you'll have the last laugh. Poke fun at yourself before you open the envelope. Before you give your acceptance speech. Before the limo pulls in front of your door. Before you walk down the aisle. Before the curtain rises. Before the meeting. Before you look in the three-way mirror. Before you check your horoscope. Before your guests arrive. And before you have to ask what's so funny about that.

Anticipate opportunities for laughter. All the world's a stage, said the Bard. The other great jester, Charlie Chaplin, explains: "All I need to make a comedy is a park, a policeman, and a pretty girl."

"I used to be Snow White, but I drifted." —Mae West

The Best of Mae West

When she was thirty-nine years old, Mae West made her first cameo appearance in a Hollywood film. She wrote her own lines for what is now a classic scene. "Goodness, what beautiful diamonds," remarked a hatcheck girl. "Goodness has nothing to do with it, dearie," West replied. Since, few women have been able to match her wit. Here is a sampling of some of her most celebrated quips.

"Every man wants to protect me. I can't figure out what from."

"When I am good I am very, very good, but when
I am bad, I am better."

"Too much of a good thing can be wonderful."

"It's not the men in my life that count, it's the life in my men."

"To err is human—but it feels divine."

"It is better to be looked over than overlooked."

"When women go wrong, men go right after them."

"It's hard to be funny when you have to be clean."

"I only like two kinds of men: domestic and foreign."

"I wrote the story myself: It's about a girl who lost
her reputation and never missed it."

10

the art of becoming

We grow up one day at a time, without ever being able to study the master plan. Some say that's how cathedrals were built—progressively, over decades or even centuries, without architects or even blueprints. In the same way, the child invents the adult he or she will become, with the final design visible only in the end.

Don't look back to find out where you are going. The answer is ahead of you. Treat your regrets, your memories, and your pearls of wisdom the way you treat your vacation snapshots. Let them gather dust. Be a precursor of who you will become later.

Instead of describing yourself as the daughter of Italian immigrants, why not say "I am the future owner of a little cabin in Montana" or "I am the favorite aunt of my three youngest nieces" or "I am the first wife of my second husband"?

But we prefer to begin our account in the past tense, with where our parents come from, what they have done, and who they became. In primitive societies, people used to be able to rattle off their long genealogy as a way to introduce themselves. Today, curiosity about where we come from still drives our sense of self.

The great narratives of the world are always told in hindsight. Even when people talk about their legacy, they try to describe it in terms of history—in terms of what others will remember after they are gone. When they should be writing the book or the symphony that would make them famous in the next century, they write their obituary.

Get a head start on the future by projecting your intuition five, twenty, or one hundred years from now. Look in the mirror and see yourself as the younger version of the person you want to be at age sixty. Treat children with the respect due the adults they will become. And think of your daughter-in-law not as the woman who married your son, but as the future grandmother of your great-grandchildren.

Too many of us adopt one life narrative, and hold its truisms to be self-evident. We assume that our awareness of a sequence of events reflects the chronologi-

Become someone you haven't met yet.

cal reality. Not so, according to contemporary historians. We are what is called in the post-modern jargon "unreliable narrators" of our own biography—subjective eyewitnesses who do not know all the facts about ourselves and thus do not grasp the full scope of their meaning.

To avoid being fooled by your own perceptions, use your imagination and take a second look at your life through the eyes of someone else—someone as different from you as possible. Try to figure out how the girl at the checkout counter sees you. How your assistant describes you to her boyfriend. Or what goes through the mind of the foreign-exchange student from China who came to dinner at your house. A composite image will emerge, revealing nuances much more subtle than anything you could have conceived on your own.

Don't be defensive by trying to correct the impression you make on others. If they admire you, don't undermine your accomplishments in front of them. If they are envious, don't apologize for your lucky breaks. Who you are to them is not about you, but about them. Be gracious and embrace the role you play in *their* narrative.

What we call a midlife crisis is usually a readjustment between conflicting narratives—between our current story line and the world in which we live. We usually respond to the situation by trying to make changes. The telltale signs are obvious: Men trim their thinning hair and get new glasses while women undergo a jewelry makeover, switching from gold to silver, or vice versa.

More than a new lifestyle, we need a new metaphor for our experience. If you don't like the way things are turning out for you, for crying out loud, fire your internal scriptwriter! Get a poet instead. Or a philosopher. Or a Zen master. Or a postmodern historian. Someone who can tell your story anew, with a fresh reinterpretation that precludes heroes and villains and convenient conclusions with moralistic overtones.

Don't squeeze all your passions, obsessions, preoccupations, and infatuations into a narrative that has a neat beginning, middle, an ending. This is you, remember? Not *Ivanhoe,* by Sir Walter Scott.

THE MYTH

We have to stop misleading our children. We owe them the truth. Sooner or later they will find out, so why keep up the charade any longer? Let's debunk the myth of youth as soon as possible.

We need volunteers right now to tell the kids that the best age to be alive is not eighteen but fifty-five.

Parents should explain to their boys and girls that the older one gets, the more fun one can have. All the games and all the toys in the world don't compare with the pleasures they will get when they are grown-ups. Playing with their friends is only practice for the serious business of having the time of their life as adults.

In other words, children should be spared the anxiety of thinking that they have to be happy while they are young. Their childhood will not be such a cruel disappointment if they know that they will have plenty of opportunities in their later years to make up for their awkward beginning.

Remember your own youth, and how much better off you would have been if you had known in advance that being young was going to be tough. You would not have been so hurt when you were sent to your room. Or so heartbroken when you had to say good-bye to your best friend at the end of the summer. Or so embarrassed when your father tried to show off by speaking French with the waiter. Or so mortified when sex was discussed in front of you.

Let's be up-front about the benefits of age. Let's break the gray wall of silence and give the next generation something exciting to look forward to.

Hang in there, kids. Getting older feels like being young at long last. Finally, you've got the zest, the ambition, and the understanding to derive an extraordinary pleasure from being the proud owner of both a body and a soul.

The Story of Your Life

As we get older, our story gets shorter. We feel that the less we say about ourselves, the more accurate we are. In some strange way, we become less than the sum of our parts.

When we are young, we need a three-page résumé to describe our degrees, our professional accomplishments, and our awards. Twenty years later, our credentials fit in a one-paragraph bio. But we've truly made it when we are identified in print by a one-sentence description.

Capture the essence of your experience by leaving out crucial details when explaining who you are and what you do.

- If you are multitalented, downplay it. Praise your children instead.
- If you are an author, omit the titles of your books. On the other hand, be sure to mention where you live.
- If you own a company, don't explain what it does, but list your clients.
- If you were born before 1960, rather than flaunt your experience, quote people half your age.
- If you are famous, don't drop names. Talk about your next project instead.
- If you are the best, don't tell others—that's what friends are for.

Sometimes it feels like the most important thing about you is the name of your cat.

"We are always the same age inside." —Gertrude Stein

You will always run into people who complain about getting older—they are usually rather young. They don't understand yet how lucky they are to have survived their youth unharmed. Give them a couple more years, though, and they will fully appreciate their good fortune.

The second part of one's life is second to nothing. Too bad we have to wait so long to get to it. If only one could grow older sooner! But so be it. When you become your adult self at last, you stop counting the years. You take possession of what you used to call your future—an invigorating now-or-never time.

Gaze ahead as you grow up. The clock of age doesn't tick for those who don't look back.

Austad, Steven N. *Why We Age*. New York: John Wiley & Sons, Inc., 1997.

Berger, John. *Ways of Seeing*. London: British Broadcasting Corporation and Penguin Books Ltd., 1972.

Fisher, Helen. *Anatomy of Love*. New York: Random House, 1992.

Fulford, Robert. *The Triumph of Narrative*. Toronto: House of Anansi Press Ltd., 1999.

Goleman, Daniel. *Healing Emotions*. Boston: Shambhala, 1997.

Hall, Edward T. *The Dance of Life*. New York: Anchor Books/Doubleday, 1983.

Hayflick, Leonard. *How and Why We Age*. New York: Ballantine Books, 1994.

Hirsch, Edward. *How to Read a Poem*. New York: Harcourt Brace and Company, 1999.

Isaacs, William. *Dialogue*. New York: Currency Books, 1999.

Levine, Robert. *A Geography of Time*. New York: Basic Books, 1997.

Medina, John J. *The Clock of Ages*. Cambridge: Cambridge University Press, 1996.

Nuland, Sherwin B. *How We Live*. New York: Vintage, 1997.

van Gennep, Arnold. *The Rites of Passage*. Chicago: The University Press of Chicago, 1960. Originally published in French in 1908.

PHOTO CREDITS

Parents, family, friends—all have added in some way to my work: encouragement, challenge, ponderings, equipment, lessons on meeting the world with observation, patience, technique and the abandonment of it all to flash on the moment.

Thank you all,
Jeanne

Jacket: Lilly, "Spanish Steps," Los Angeles. Title page: Victoria, New York. Introduction: Musée d'Orsay, Paris.

Page 11: Cynthia's music stand, New York. Page 12: Door at sunset, Provence, France. Page 17: Rope banister, Roquemengarde, Languedoc, France. Page 18: Pont Alexandre III, Paris.

Page 21: Lunch with Kirsten and Desmond, La Jolla, California. Page 22: Cleaning up after Grand-papa's eightieth birthday party, Montmartre, Paris. Page 26: Merry-go-round, Trocadéro, Paris.

Page 29: Antique clock, Paris. Page 31: Colette at the wheel of her new "Smart." Page 33: Florence, Place Saint-Sulpice, Paris.

Page 37: Cats, ancient and modern, New York. Page 38: Grade-school friends Edith and Cynthia, New York. Page 42: Michael's office, Shekomeko, New York.

Page 45: Cathedral chairs, Rheims, France. Page 47: Lexa and Peter, Hanukkah, New York. Page 50: Karen at home, New York.

Page 53: Dancing to Zydeco, Kirsten, Michael, and Desmond, Ruston, Louisiana. Page 54: "Sunday Soup," Lilly, Los Angeles. Page 58: Philippe in SoHo, New York.

Page 61: Two paths, Azay-le-Rideau, France. Page 65: Shelley and Madison, Brooklyn, New York. Page 66: Evita with chickens, Shekomeko, New York.

Page 69: Jean-Jacques, Véronique, and Bill at L'Acajou, New York. Page 70: Fourteen for dinner, New York. Page 74: Dodonna in Wyoming.

Page 77: Nelly, Raymonde, and Hélène, Paris. Page 78: Leo, Sara, and Marc, Paris. Page 82: After the blizzard of '95, Brooklyn, New York.

Page 85: Madeleine, Los Angeles. Page 87: Carl in his studio, New York. Page 90: Moomoon and Véronique, Brooklyn, New York.

Page 92: Rainy day, Palais Royal, Paris. Page 95: Home office, Montmartre, Paris.